The 23rd Psalm

The 23rd Psalm

SELWYN HUGHES

Published by CWR, Waverley Abbey House, Waverley Lane, Farnham, Surrey
GU9 8EP
Copyright © 2001 by Selwyn Hughes
First published in Great Britain 1986 in illustrated format. Revised edition
2001.
ISBN 1 85345 192 4
Design and typesetting: Christine Reissland and Elaine Bond at CWR
Creative Services
Printed in England by Linney Print
Photos: PhotoDisc, Eddie Tait, Digital Stock Corporation, Roger Walker,
CCD, PhotoAlto
Front cover images: PhotoDisc

Introduction

Psalm 23 is well known and loved, even by those who know very little else of the Bible. For some it is simply a beautiful piece of prose for weddings and funerals. But in this devotional book we explore the psalm phrase by phrase.

David is believed to have written this psalm after fleeing into the wilderness. This is a passage for those who are experiencing some major upheaval in life. I assure you that when you really absorb the truths buried in this psalm, you need never again be overwhelmed by life's valleys.

Use the lessons from this book to ask yourself some key questions: "Do I really know the Lord described in Psalm 23?"; "How do I see God?"; "Is He my Loving Shepherd or harsh judge?"

I hope that through this meditation Psalm 23 will come alive in a whole new way. I pray that you will see the reality of all that the Shepherd does for us, His precious sheep. We are safe with Him, we are secure.

This is a book to use as a prayerful meditation on the Lord, on our understanding of Him and His amazing and practical love for us. Understand that the bonds between us and the Shepherd are so strong that nothing can ever separate us.

Selwyn Hughes

"A nightingale among birds"

One of the most beautiful and best-loved passages in the whole of God's Word is the twenty-third Psalm. This serene and sacred psalm towers over the others as does Mount Everest over the Himalayas. The great preacher C.H. Spurgeon said of it: "What the nightingale is among birds, this psalm is among others; it has sung sweetly in the ear of many a dejected soul, and in the night of his weeping has given him hope for a morning of joy."

Psalm 23:1–6

Many have memorised this exquisite psalm, but have never given the time to study it in detail. Commentators believe that it was written during the time when David's son Absalom rebelled against him, causing him to flee into the wilderness of Judea. Outlawed and hunted, David solaced himself with images drawn from his more peaceful days as a shepherd.

Psalm 23 is a passage that particularly speaks to people who, like David, are experiencing a major upheaval in life.

Do you feel let down by someone who has been extremely close to you? Have the skies suddenly become overcast and grey? Is a longstanding friendship about to break up? Then this psalm is for you. Begin memorising it and repeating it out loud to yourself. Roll every word around on the tip of your spiritual tongue and suck every precious drop of refreshment from it. Let it lie upon your mind until you feel its peace and serenity invading and penetrating every cell of your being. I promise you that if you will make the effort to absorb the truths that lie buried in this matchless psalm, you will never again be overwhelmed by life's difficulties and problems.

David begins by putting his problems in their proper context – he focuses his gaze directly upon God: "The Lord is my shepherd". Have you learned yet how to get your spiritual focus right when caught up in a crisis? If you don't immediately bring God into the problem, then you have no proper frame of reference in which to deal with your difficulties. Someone has said, "If we haven't that within us which is above us, we will soon yield to that which is around us."

Psalm 18:1–50

I feel immensely sorry for those who do not know God and have to face their troubles alone. An agnostic professor spoke for all who share his agnosticism when he wrote: "I am not sure whether my doings have anything cosmic at the back of them, whether I am working with anything significant, or just working meaninglessly alone, with no one to back my work or care." No wonder someone described both agnostics and atheists as "people who have no invisible means of support".

How different situations look – even desperate situations – when God is brought into the picture. Instead of being tossed about on wave after wave of inane existence, we have a star by which we can steer our boat – and a safe and certain harbour. David puts his problems in the right context by saying, "Look at who my Shepherd is – the Lord of glory!" When we pause in the midst of our problems to reflect on who is guiding us, we will say, like David: "The Lord! He is my Shepherd."

Once David has set the context in which to consider his situation and circumstances, he goes on to focus on the relationship that exists between himself and God: the Lord is *my* Shepherd. Obviously David has no doubts about his personal relationship with the divine Shepherd, and is thrilled to belong to Him. Permit me to ask you this personal question: Do you know the Lord in an intimate way? Can you say, as did David: the Lord is *my* Shepherd?

Isaiah 42:1–7

Perhaps one of the saddest situations which occurs in life is to hear so many recite Psalm 23 without having a personal relationship with the One of whom it so tenderly speaks. A great actor was once asked to recite something in a small social gathering, and he decided upon Psalm 23. He recited the words with perfect diction and tone, and his performance was followed by great applause. An old minister who was present asked if he, too, could be permitted to recite the same psalm. Although it soon became obvious that he lacked the skill and professionalism of the actor, and though he stumbled and faltered over some of the words, there was not a dry eye in the audience by the time he had finished.

Someone who was there described the difference in the audience's reactions in this way: "The actor knew the psalm, but the minister knew the Shepherd." So I ask you again: do you really belong to Him? Do you live under His daily direction and control? Knowing the psalm is one thing – hearsay – but knowing the Shepherd is quite another – heartsay. If you do not know Him in this personal way, then I urge you – surrender your life to Him this very moment.

Our primary view of God

Why did David choose to think of God as his Shepherd? The picture of God we carry deep in our hearts is the one we relate to whenever we find ourselves surrounded by trouble or difficulties. But perhaps what is more important is this – we will interpret every event of our lives in accordance with the inner picture that we have of Him.

I have referred before to the fact that, when I have asked people during counselling to describe to me their primary view of God, I have been surprised that so often they see Him, not as a loving Shepherd but as an austere and stern Judge. God is a Judge, of course – as David discovered when he committed adultery with Bathsheba – but that is not His primary relationship to His children. Someone has pointed out that the two most beautiful illustrations of God's relationship to His people given in Scripture are those of a Father and a Shepherd. It is interesting also that the two best-known passages in the whole of God's Word – the Lord's Prayer and Psalm 23 – use these analogies.

What kind of picture of God, I wonder, do you carry deep down in your heart? If your primary view of God is as a Judge, then you will tend to interpret your problems as God's judgment upon you, rather than an opportunity to experience in your troubles His tender love and care. Make no mistake about it – the image of God that you carry deep in your heart is the one that you will relate to in a moment of crisis.

Psalm 80;
Psalm 95;
Psalm 100

David, in the midst of his trials, consoled himself with the thought that God was not his Judge, but his Shepherd. This was his primary view of God, and thus the image of the divine Shepherd's tender love and care filled his heart as he meditated upon Him.

Someone once said: "You will never rise higher in your Christian life and experience than your image and concept of God." How true. You see, you can recite the words of Psalm 23 all day, but it will not have much effect if the picture of God you carry deep in your heart is that of a tyrant or a despot. Your wrong image of God will negate the impact of the words. Archbishop William Temple put it like this: "It is not so much the words we say with our lips that produce inner peace, but the thoughts that we carry deep within our heart. It is down there – in the heart – that the real changes take place. If the thoughts in our hearts do not really correspond with the words on our lips, then we are just whistling in the dark."

So before we go any further into this simple, yet profoundly beautiful psalm, check on how true to Scripture your primary picture of God is. Is He tender – or tyrannical? Caring – or condemning? A negative view of God is rarely changed overnight, but I am confident that as we meditate upon this transforming psalm, we shall

finally come to the same conclusion as David – that everything that a good shepherd is to his sheep, God is to His people.

As we have been meditating on the phrase, "The Lord is my shepherd", we have seen the importance of gaining a clear concept of who God is, or, as someone once said, "the clearer your concept of God, the more vital will be your relationship with Him". How clear is your concept of God? Can you say, as did David, "the Lord is my shepherd"?

John 10:1–18

Psalm 23 has been described by someone as "David's hymn of praise to divine diligence". The entire passage recounts the way in which the divine Shepherd spares no

pains for the welfare of His sheep. No wonder David, previously a shepherd himself, took pride in being a member of God's flock.

The Christian writer, Phillip Keller, tells how he spent some years managing a sheep ranch and makes reference to a shepherd he knew who was completely indifferent to the needs of the sheep. "The man," he says, "gave little or no time to his flock, letting them pretty well forage for themselves as best they could, both in summer and winter. They fell prey to dogs, cougars and rustlers. They had only polluted, muddy water to drink. In my mind's eye I can see still them standing at the fence, huddled sadly in little knots, staring wistfully through the wires at the rich pastures on the other side."

That shepherd ignored the needs of his sheep – he couldn't have cared less. How different is the divine Shepherd. For Him there is no greater joy, no richer reward, no deeper satisfaction than that of seeing His sheep safe, contented and flourishing under His care.

No matter what . . .

Isaiah 40:1–11

We turn now to the next phrase which David utters as he encourages himself in God: "The Lord is my shepherd, I shall not want" (AV).

What a bold and positive statement to make! At first glance, however, the words seem quite absurd. Here is David in the midst of intense privation, hunted and hounded by hostile enemy forces, deserted by many of his former supporters – yet quietly affirming, "I shall not want". In the past I have known many Christians who have had great difficulty in understanding this phrase. They have said, "How can I recite this verse with any meaning when I want so many things? I want a happy family/ better living conditions/an adequate supply of money/employment/a wife/a husband" and so on.

The meaning of what David is saying here becomes clear when we dig a little deeper into the original Hebrew words that are used. One translation says: "I shall lack nothing." Another puts it like this: "I shall not lack any good thing." "The main thought," says one commentator, "is that of not lacking – not being deficient – in proper care, management or husbandry."

So what David is really saying is this: no matter what hardships or privations come my way, I am confident of this one thing – that I shall not lack the expert care and tender supervision of my Master and my Shepherd. There were many things that David lacked – he lacked the comforts of life, family affection, physical security, and so on. What he did not lack, however, was the assurance that God was with him in his difficulties, managing his affairs and turning all his stumbling-blocks into stepping stones.

If we accept that Psalm 23 was written during the time of David's sojourn in the wilderness of Judea, then he could not have been referring to material or physical benefits, for quite clearly he was bereft of them. The obvious conclusion, then, is that David, in making this statement, is boasting in the fact that no matter what hardship he might endure, he would never want – never lack – the expert care and management of his tender, loving Shepherd.

Psalm 73:1–28

Putting back
the perspective

It is at this point that we must take a long, hard look at reality, for there are many who believe that once we become Christians, we ought to be exempt from the ordinary ills that afflict humanity. Those who adopt this attitude go down like ninepins when trouble strikes. A woman who had been overtaken by a series of difficult problems said to me on one occasion: "Why should this happen to me? I'm a Christian. God should treat me better." I pointed out that the attitude she was adopting was highly dangerous, but I am afraid my words did not make much impression. She finished up in a serious nervous condition which required several months of hospital treatment.

Richard Baxter wrote of the Great Plague, "At first so few religious people were taken away that they began to be puffed up and boast of the great differences which God did make. But quickly after that they all fell alike." What, then, is the difference between a Christian and a non-Christian? The difference is not in what happens to us, but what we are able to do with what happens.

Difficulties and problems come to all of us – Christians and non-Christians alike. But while the same things happen to us all, they do not have the same effect upon us all. The same thing happening to two different people may have an entirely different effect. It all depends on our inner attitudes. As someone has said: "What life does to us in the long run depends on what life finds in us."

Psalm 121:1–8

During a counselling session, a man said, "I have found a verse in the Bible that describes my life perfectly." He picked up a Bible that was lying on the desk and opened it at Job 5:7. "Here, read that – aloud," he said to the counsellor. The counsellor read: "Man is born to trouble as surely as sparks fly upward." "I was born to trouble," complained the counsellee. "I live in trouble and I'll probably die in trouble. There's always a new burst of sparks, and they are burning me something awful."

The counsellor, with a flash of divine insight, said, "There's another verse which accurately describes your life also: it's 1 Peter 5:7." Then, handing him the Bible, he said: "Now you read it – aloud." The man read these thrilling words: "Cast all your anxiety on him because he cares for you." He was silent for a time, and then, with a tear trickling down his cheek, said, "Thank you for putting the perspective back into my life. I needed a word from God and He has given it to me through you today." I wonder – is this also His word to you?

"Listening posts"

W e are seeing that the phrase "I shall not want" (AV) does not mean that we are exempt from the ordinary ills and troubles of life, but that in the midst of those troubles we experience our Shepherd's expert management and care. Comb the record of the Scriptures and you find, time and time again, that when God's servants were caught up in periods of great difficulty and distress, they knew that He had not abandoned them but was working out His purposes with infinite tenderness and skill.

Take, for example, the apostle John. He says: "I ... found myself in the island called Patmos, for adhering to God's word and the testimony of Jesus ... I found myself rapt in the Spirit and I heard a loud voice ..." (Rev. 1:9–10, Moffatt). He was isolated and bereft of human companionship and care – but was he bereft of the care and companionship of his Master? Assuredly not! Listen again to what he says: "I found myself in the island called Patmos ... and I heard." Shut off from men, he was more open to God.

1 Kings 19:1–18

Islands of isolation are good "listening posts". Shut off from the clamouring voices of the world, you can hear God more easily. Just recently I leafed through an old Bible which I had discarded, and I was intrigued to see that I had written a date against certain Bible verses. Only the Lord and I know what happened on those dates, but I can tell you that they were times when I felt utterly barren and isolated. Today I can bear witness to the fact that the Good Shepherd, with characteristic skill, used those moments to speak to me in a way that I have never forgotten. My prayer is that He will do the same for you.

Away from the clamouring voices of the world, John was able to hear God's voice more easily.

Much later in the book of Revelation we read this: "So he bore me away rapt in the Spirit to the desert, and there I saw …" (Rev. 17:3, Moffatt). John is now not only on an isolated island: he is in a desert on the island. In addition to the isolation – there was barrenness. Sometimes our isolations are more than we can bear, but when they are accompanied by barrenness – life borders on the intolerable. Let us not forget, however, that our Shepherd will never allow us to get into any position in which He cannot work for our good and for His own eternal glory.

Listen to the words again: "So he bore me away … to the desert … and there I saw". "Saw" what? The downfall of the empires of the world! In the isolated and barren periods of life we may be able to do or contribute little, but we can see God do much – indeed everything. And in the end, does it matter all that much whether we do things, or see God do them? We sometimes think we and our efforts are indispensable. Our work is important – but dispensable. Union and fellowship with God are what really matter. John might have thought to himself, as he was left alone on Patmos: "There's not much future in this place!" Yet he finished up by seeing the whole future of mankind. Take it from me, when your present offers you little on your island of isolation, your Master will see that the future will offer you everything.

Deuteronomy
32:10–14

The Shepherd
is near

Having seen that, no matter what our circumstances, we are never bereft of our Shepherd's supervision and care, we turn now to focus on the next phrase of this beautiful and exquisite psalm: "He makes me lie down in green pastures".

Phillip Keller, the Christian writer and one-time shepherd to whom I referred earlier, explains that sheep are extremely timid animals by nature, and cannot be made to lie down unless four requirements are met. They will not lie down until they are (1) free from all fear; (2) free from friction with the other sheep; (3) free from torment by flies and parasites, and (4) free from the pangs of hunger. Obviously, it depends on the diligence of the shepherd as to whether or not his flock is free from these disturbing influences.

The very first thing a shepherd does in order to calm and reassure his sheep is to make them aware of his presence. *The Handbook of Bible Times and Customs* states: "Nothing puts a flock of sheep more at ease than to see their shepherd walking in the field." Isn't it just the same in the Christian life? I don't know about you, but whenever I am beset by troubles and trials the thing that quietens and reassures my spirit is the keen awareness that my Shepherd is nearby. There is nothing like Christ's presence to dispel the tension, the panic and the terror of the unknown. Perhaps at this very moment you are facing a tragedy or a crisis that threatens to send shock waves of fear through your whole being. Take heart – your Shepherd is not far away. His presence in the situation makes a world of difference.

So one of the ways in which the Good Shepherd delivers us from fear is by making us keenly aware of His loving presence.

Psalm 16:1–11

When I was a young child, I was terrified of thunder. If I was out on the street when a thunderstorm occurred, I would hide in a doorway, terror stricken. When a thunderstorm came in the middle of the night, however, I had little fear because I knew that automatically my mother would come into my room, get into bed with me, and stay there all night to make me feel safe. Now, whenever I read the verse that is before us today – "perfect love drives out fear" – I cannot help but think of my mother slipping into bed with me during a thunderstorm. Her loving presence made all the difference between calmness and fear.

1 John 4:9–21

When we are conscious that we are loved, deeply loved, then fear dissolves as readily as the morning mist before the rising sun. Fear can only come where love is not – and where love is, fear is not. Some try to get rid of their fears by drowning themselves in alcohol. But next morning the fears are back – multiplied. Others try to deal with their fears by pushing them down into the unconscious and pretending they are not there. This, too, is ineffective. The way to deal with fear is to focus more on Christ than you do on your fear. You see, you become like the thing on which you focus. Focus on fear – and you cannot help but become perturbed. Focus on Christ and you cannot help but be at peace. Keep your eyes fixed on your Shepherd – and you will soon be convinced that there is really nothing to fear.

Friction in the flock

The second source of conflict from which a good shepherd seeks to deliver his sheep is tension, rivalry and competition within the flock itself. I am given to understand that just as there is a "pecking order" among chickens, so there is a "butting order" among sheep. This thought is brought out very vividly in Ezekiel 34. Rival tension, competition for status and self-assertion can produce a great deal of friction in a flock – the sheep are unable to lie down and rest in contentment.

Unfortunately there are many churches like this. Men and women fight and compete among themselves for position or status and thus create conflict in the Christian community. The apostle James says of them that they "crave for something and don't get it ... are jealous and envious of what others have got and ... in exasperated frustration struggle and fight with one another" (James 4:2, J.B. Phillips). Many are prevented from enjoying the blessings of corporate fellowship because of the competitiveness and status-seeking of a few.

How does a shepherd deal with friction among his sheep? He does it by walking among them to discipline the offenders and reassure those that are alarmed. A good shepherd has great compassion for the sheep that get butted and pushed around by the more domineering ones. Is your church or fellowship in conflict because of over-competitive and status-seeking Christians? Then make sure your eyes stay focused on the divine Shepherd. He will discipline them and reassure you.

Ezekiel
34:11–24

Overcoming irritations

The third cause of disturbance from which a shepherd seeks to deliver his sheep is that which comes from marauding insects – flies and ticks.

Sheep, especially during the hot season, can be driven almost to distraction by these winged invaders. At such times it is quite impossible for the shepherd to make them lie down: they remain on their feet, stamp their legs, shake their heads and are ready to rush off in any direction to find relief. A diligent shepherd can do several things to help his sheep overcome these irritations. He can make sure, for example, that they are regularly dipped, so that their fleeces are cleared of ticks. And he can see to it that they are put out to graze in areas where there is plenty of shade.

We now ask ourselves: how does our Good Shepherd go about the task of helping His sheep overcome the irritations that beset them? What is the remedy He uses to help us come to a place of quiet contentment and repose? The answer is this – divine grace! The apostle Paul, in 2 Corinthians 12:7 tells of experiencing a "thorn in my flesh". What it was nobody quite knows. Eye disease, epilepsy, an unrelenting Satanic attack – each has been suggested. But still nobody is certain. One writer, commenting on this, says: "Paul had a thorn in the flesh but nobody knows what it was: if we had a thorn in the flesh everybody would know what it was." Paul tells us he sought three times for its removal – yet it remained. At last, however, came the comforting word: "My grace is sufficient for you". God's grace enabled Paul to cope with his irritation and, believe me, that same grace will enable you to cope with yours.

2 Corinthians
12:1–10

Freedom
from hunger

We come now to the fourth and final condition which is necessary before a sheep can lie down contentedly – freedom from hunger. This fact, of course, is clearly implied in the words: "He makes me lie down in green pastures."

Nothing delights a shepherd as much as seeing his sheep well and truly fed, for it is only then that they will lie down to rest and ruminate. One eastern shepherd makes this comment: "Whenever I see one of my sheep moving around discontentedly, always on its feet, looking here, there and everywhere, I know that sheep is hungry. And hungry sheep do not thrive. I make it my goal to immediately try to ascertain what is wrong, for I know that unless the matter is soon rectified, the sheep will languish and lack vigour and vitality."

A shepherd sometimes has to work extremely hard to bring his sheep into "green pastures". He has to go ahead of his sheep and reconnoitre the best grazing areas, then plan how to get them safely to the spot he has selected – all of which requires unrelenting energy and determination. And some times, when all of this has been accomplished and the sheep are safely settled in "green pastures", a shepherd will spy one or more of the sheep nibbling at inferior forage instead of enjoying the lush pasture that he has provided. Every shepherd says that it is a disappointing and frustrating moment. How does the divine Shepherd feel, I wonder, when, after having supplied the "green pastures" of His Word on which we may feed, we attempt to live day by day off the barren ground of the world around us?

Isaiah 55:1–13

"Still waters"

The next phrase that occurs in "David's hymn of praise to divine diligence" is "He leads me beside still waters"(AV). One cannot help but notice how the varied needs of the sheep and the many-sided care of the shepherd are pictured with consummate skill in the short sentences of this psalm.

When I was researching this theme, I came across a small booklet which was sent to me by a friend several years ago entitled "The Song of the Syrian quest". It is a brief analysis of Psalm 23 from the viewpoint of a Syrian shepherd, and in it he makes this illuminating comment: "So many things familiar to us are strange to you who come from the West. When you read the words, 'He leads me beside still waters', you think of quietly flowing streams, but streams are few and far between in the Middle East and the shepherds do not rely upon them. Sheep are afraid of fast-running water; they will drink only from a quiet pool. The 'still waters' are the wells and cisterns, and the shepherd leads his sheep to these still waters so that he may draw water and quench their thirst."

What a deeply impressive and suggestive picture this is of the way in which the divine Shepherd leads us day by day to the quiet waters of spiritual refreshment. Pause for a moment now; read John 7:37–38, then close your eyes if possible and focus on this passage. Allow the Good Shepherd to prepare you for what lies ahead, to slake your spiritual thirst, and refresh your soul with His eternal Word.

John 7:37–38

How, in an age of turmoil and strife, can we discover those "still waters" of which the Bible so eloquently speaks? The answer is found in the Quiet Time. A Quiet Time – a concept that unfortunately seems to be missing in the lives of many modern-day Christians – is a time, preferably at the beginning of the day, when we meet with God in prayer and the reading of the Scriptures.

Lamentations
3:19–40

One of the things that concerns me about many young Christians today is the fact that they are not taught to begin the day with God. Much of this, I know, is a reaction against the legalism that pervaded the Church a few decades ago, when many Bible teachers suggested that if you missed your daily Quiet Time – for any reason at all – you were in danger of losing your soul. Nowadays – generally speaking – we seem to have swung to the other extreme, regarding a daily Quiet Time as unimportant and irrelevant.

The simple truth is that if we do not provide for a Quiet Time at the beginning of the day, we will most likely have to provide for an unquiet time throughout the day. A diver who is too busy to make sure his air supply is working before he descends into the depths is no more foolish than the Christian who descends into the murky waters of today's world without getting his spiritual breathing apparatus connected up with the pure air of the kingdom of God.

If you are too busy to have a daily Quiet Time, then, quite frankly, you are too busy. The probabilities are that you will have to take time off during the day to deal with issues that you might have more easily foreseen had you begun the day with God. Let me make clear once again that I am not advocating a legalistic attitude to this issue, for there are some days when circumstances make it quite impossible to keep to a routine. But as far as possible, begin every day by spending a little time with God in prayer and the reading of His Word.

Psalm 5:1–12

One shepherd described his feelings of exasperation when, taking his sheep to a clean, quiet stream to be watered, he found many of them stopping to drink from small, dirty, muddy pools beside the trail. "The water in these pools was filthy and polluted", said the shepherd, "but the sheep were quite sure it was the best drink obtainable." How sad that so many Christians are like those stubborn sheep – they stop to drink at any stream except the pure waters of God's eternal and inerrant Word. From what source do you draw your spiritual strength?

I asked a man who was living a defeated Christian life if he kept a daily Quiet Time and the naive reply came: "Yes, I spend ten to fifteen minutes every day reading Shakespeare. Another couple said that their idea of a Quiet Time was to quietly sit and read the newspaper for half an hour after breakfast. These sincere but defeated souls found release and victory when they set up a real Quiet Time, in which they took on board the quietening and quickening resources of God. Shakespeare and the daily newspaper may make interesting reading, but they are poor and pitiable substitutes for the Word of God.

"An island within"

Some Bible teachers maintain that Spirit-filled Christians don't need to cultivate a Quiet Time. They say: "If you are filled with the Spirit, then you can draw from God's resources, not just at the beginning of the day, but every hour of the day. Better a fountain in the heart than a fountain by the way."

This confuses two quite separate issues. It is perfectly true that by reason of the Spirit's indwelling, we can draw upon His resources moment by moment, but that does not do away with the need for a daily Quiet Time. One writer puts it like this. "Those who say they can live in a state of prayer without stated times for prayer will probably find themselves without both. It is as futile as thinking that you can live in a state of physical nourishment without stated times for nourishment."

Psalm
119:137–152

I believe with all my heart that the divine Shepherd seeks daily to lead His sheep to the "quiet waters" of His Word, and how sad it is that so many Christians prefer to drink from the polluted pools of the world. The poet says:

What a frail soul He gave me, and a heart
Lame and unlikely for the large events.

I wonder if, more often, we haven't given ourselves "a heart lame and unlikely for the large events". God has given us infinite resources through prayer and the reading of the Scriptures. They are ours for the asking and the taking. The Quiet Time creates an island of quiet within us, and that becomes the atmosphere of the day.

The Bible should be at the heart of every Quiet Time. I knew a Christian who believed in the importance of a Quiet Time but unfortunately had a very low estimate of Scripture and saw no necessity for its use in his meditations. He thought he could get to God direct – through the medium of his own conceptions. His conceptions, however, were Man's thoughts about God – not a good enough medium for communication with the Eternal. He finished up by going off at a tangent and getting involved in a false cult.

Unless our thoughts are constantly corrected by God's thoughts, they will either go off at a tangent or become sterile and unproductive. The Bible is God's revelation of Himself, and the more we meditate in it the clearer our minds will become concerning the nature of God and His purpose for our lives. I consider the content of *Every Day with Jesus* to be exhausted after it has been read through once – hence the fresh supply. But you can never exhaust the meaning of the Scriptures. Don't, I beg you, be like those who walk in their own ways and drink from the polluted pools of the world. Let the Lord lead you daily to the "still waters" of His Word. Then, and only then, will you know a serenity of soul in the midst of life's turmoils and difficulties.

Hebrews 4:1–13

2 Timothy 3:14–17

"Cast down" and restored

Isaiah 42:1–16

The next phrase we come to in this beautiful and exquisite psalm is this: "He restores my soul". What a comforting and encouraging statement this is! Here again, it points to the constant care of the Good Shepherd who is set on providing the fullest protection and security for His sheep.

What we must continually keep in mind as we go through this psalm is that David is not speaking here as a shepherd, though he was one, but as a sheep – one of the flock. After all, he knew from firsthand experience that the welfare of any particular sheep depended to a great degree on the type of shepherd who owned it. But what does David have in mind when he exclaims: "He restores my soul"?

The phrase is open to many interpretations. Some believe it has reference to the way in which God comes to us when we feel cast down and sets us up on our feet again, so to speak. It's interesting that the phrase "cast down" is an old English shepherd's term for a sheep that has turned over on its back and can't get up again by itself. If this happens, and the shepherd does not arrive on the scene within a reasonably short time, the sheep panics and can easily die of fright.

Are you feeling "cast down" at this moment? Well, take heart – the author of this psalm knew that experience too. In Psalm 42:11 he cries out: "Why are you cast down, O my soul, and why are you disquieted within me? Hope in God ..." (RSV). Notice that last phrase – "hope in God". That's the secret. The divine Shepherd will not let you down. Look up – for even now He is moving towards you. He will pick you up and put you back on your feet again.

"A 'cast' sheep is a very pathetic sight", says Phillip Keller. "Lying on its back, its feet in the air, it flays away, frantically struggling to stand up without success. Sometimes it will bleat a little for help, but generally it lies there lashing about in frightened frustration."

He goes on to say that whenever a shepherd finds that a sheep is missing, his first thought is this: my sheep may

be cast down somewhere – I must go in search of it and set it on its feet again. "Some of my most poignant memories," he continues, "are wrapped around the co-mingled anxiety of keeping a count of my flock and repeatedly saving and restoring cast sheep."

The care and concern that the one-time shepherd, Phillip Keller, had for his sheep pales into insignificance, however, beside that of our Lord Jesus Christ. Many Christians hold the view that when they fall by the way or fail in their Christian experience, God becomes extremely angry with them. Not so. The revelation of Scripture is that Eternal God, the Almighty, the Lord of all creation has a shepherd's heart. He is infinitely more caring and compassionate toward the sheep of His fold than any human shepherd could ever be. Reflect again on the tender and loving manner in which Jesus restored Peter after he had three times denied Him. The tenderness, the compassion and the patience He showed in restoring Simon Peter are just the same as He will show in restoring you.

Luke 22:54–62;
John 21:15–19

"Draws me
back into His way"

Now that we have looked at one interpretation of the phrase, "He restores my soul", we move on to consider another.

The Syrian shepherd we mentioned earlier, Faduel Moghabghad, claims that the statement has reference to the fact that in shepherd country there are many private gardens and vineyards, and if a sheep wanders into one of these private plots, it is forfeited to the owner of the land. In his view, therefore, the phrase "He restores my soul" has reference to the way the divine Shepherd brings us back and rescues us when we stray into forbidden and dangerous places. One of our hymns, you might remember, contains some lines that reinforce this view:

Ephesians
4:17–32

> *Put His loving arms around me*
> *Drew me back into His way.*

How encouraging to know that when, by our heedlessness, and inattention to God's ways, we stray into Satan's domain, the divine Shepherd does not leave us to our own devices, but constantly seeks our deliverance and restoration.

James 1:13–14;
1 Corinthians
10:13

We must be careful at this point not to press the analogy of a sheep too far, or else we will come out believing that when we wander from the fold, it is solely the Shepherd's responsibility to seek us out and bring us back. We have some responsibility too – the responsibility to confess our sin and to be willing and ready to be

restored. We can be assured of this, God will always be willing to restore if we are willing to be restored.

Sheep wander and get lost for many reasons, but mainly through heedlessness and inattention.

Some of us get lost the same way. Like sheep, we take a series of steps, none of them seemingly important, but each one increasing our distance from the Shepherd. We go with the crowd to the hinterland of evil, expecting to

stay inwardly aloof while being outwardly near. Soon,
however, the temptation becomes too great for us, our
defences crumble, and we rationalise the issues until evil,
which before looked hideous, becomes first bearable, then
inviting, then desirable. How many times have we said to
ourselves: "But everybody does it – what's the point of
being different?" Or a series of neglects takes place: "I'm
too busy now to have a Quiet Time – I'll begin next
week." Or: "This duty is pressing – but I'll make sure it is   1 John 2:1–17
done tomorrow." "Action turns into attitude, attitude turns
into habit, habit turns into character."

A Christian once said to me: "I didn't intend to get
into this mess spiritually. I just let things slip, and now that
I need my faith it seems to have gone." How easy it is to
find ourselves in Satan's territory, not because of deliberate
intention, but through a series of inattentions. "The
descent to hell," said someone, "is so gradual that many do
not suspect the road they are following is a downward
path." The little tufts of worldliness that lure us on will,
unless we are careful, leave us lost and forlorn.

Run-down souls

We have examined two different interpretations of the phrase: "He restores my soul". Now we examine another interpretation – the one which claims that these words have reference to the way God ministers to us when we become spiritually debilitated. Personally, this is the view I find most satisfying. Life has a tendency to run down, to get jaded and ragged at the edges, tired and lacking in zest.

A sample of the kind of thing I mean is found in a letter I once received: "I'm worn down by my circumstances … tired of the pressures … wearied by the constant demands that are being made upon me. Can God do anything for me in this situation?" I was happy to respond that He can! The Good Shepherd can step into our lives when we feel tired and jaded, and provided we let Him, quickly restore our spiritual zest and enthusiasm.

Jeremiah 30:12–22

In one place in the New Testament, our Saviour is described as a stimulator: "By all the stimulus of Christ" (Phil. 2:1, Moffatt). Those who know nothing of Christ's stimulus — His ability to restore tired and jaded souls — are forced to turn to other stimulants to tide them over. Listen to the way that a famous missionary to India describes Christ's ministry of spiritual restoration: "He is like the first rainfall of the monsoon in India — the dry, dusty ground, so barren and so hard, the very next day has a green film of vegetation over it. The moisture apparently touches the dead soil, and lo, it is alive. So Jesus touches our parched and barren lives, and lo, they sprout with life, with vitality and with hope." May you know the wonder of His restoring touch this very moment.

"All we like sheep ..."

Warren focus now on the next phrase in David's "hymn of praise to divine diligence": "He guides me in paths of righteousness for his name's sake". One translation puts it: "He leads me in the paths that are right". Another says: "He leads me in the right way".

Proverbs
4:10–19

The Hebrew word for "paths" means "well-defined or clearly-marked trails". Sheep, as everyone knows, are stubborn and self-willed creatures. If left to themselves, they will almost invariably leave a well-defined trail and wander off in a direction of their own choosing. An experienced shepherd, of course, is well aware of this, and tries to offset this tendency by going ahead of his sheep and making himself as visible as possible.

We, too, are stubborn and self-willed creatures – we prefer to go our own way and do our own thing. "All we like sheep have gone astray; we have turned every one to his own way" (Isa. 53:6, RSV). As someone has said: "It is by no mere whim on God's part that He has called us sheep. Our behaviour patterns and life habits are so much like those of a sheep that it is well-nigh embarrassing." This desire that we have for self-determination, however,

has got to be curbed or else the results will be disastrous. The prophet Micah said: "O shepherd, guide thy people, thine own flock, so lonely, lonely like a wild patch within a garden" (Micah 7:14, Moffatt). The universe around us is orderly because it obeys God and follows the will of its Creator – it is a garden. When we obey ourselves, rather than God, then we are a wild patch of disorderliness within that garden of orderliness.

We prefer our own way even though it may lead us straight into trouble.

When challenged about this issue, many of us, of course, strongly deny it. Yet in actual fact, comparatively few of God's people follow continually in His path. We say: "I want to do God's will and be led by Him in all that I do" – and then promptly proceed to follow our own self-determined desires. We sing beautiful hymns and choruses that contain such words as: "The Lord knows the way through the wilderness, all I have to do is follow" – then take the path that we think is best.

This is an issue that we must come to grips with right now, for unless we learn how to give up our self-centredness, we will fall into serious trouble – no matter how loving and concerned is our Shepherd. I recognise that this is a difficult issue for many Christians, for our civilisation teaches us self-interest as the primary motivating force in life – "every man for himself and the devil take the hindmost". Actually if self-interest is primary then the result is self-destruction, for the self-centred soon become the self-disrupted. They are making themselves God, and they are not God, so the universe won't back their way of life. They are like the ones referred to in Micah: " ... so lonely, lonely like a wild patch within a garden."

Proverbs
14:1–15

Only one way

We are seeing that when we try to follow our way instead of the way into which the divine Shepherd wants to lead us, we finish up self-defeated and self-disrupted. As one writer puts it: "If you won't live according to God's way, you can't live with yourself."

A cartoon I once saw shows a doctor taking the pulse of a very sick world. He shakes his head and says: "You are in a bad way – you are allergic to yourself." You see, if you insist on going your own way, and self-interest and self-concern become the driving force of your being, then you will eventually be driven into conflict with yourself. You will find yourself with all kinds of problems and complexes – you will be allergic to yourself.

Psalm 40:1–17

A woman once said to me: "I've insisted upon having my own way all my life, but now I am middle-aged it has caught up with me. I'm empty, incapable of accomplishing anything." You can get away with having your own way for a while, but in the end it will catch up with you – that which is whispered in the ear will be shouted from the housetops (Matt. 10:27). A Christian who has never learned to go God's way rather than his own way gets nowhere – and everybody can see it. Jesus penetratingly said: "... For whoever wants to save his life will lose it" (Luke 9:24). Notice, He did not say, "whoever saves his life will lose it", but "whoever wants to save his life will lose it". He wants to save it, but he loses it – it goes to pieces. Why? Because the law of the universe decrees it. Life will not back the person who refuses to take God's way for his way is not the Way.

Our desire for self-determination has got to be curbed, or else it will lead us into ways that are not the Way. "One of the characteristics of a radiant Christian", says J. Oswald Smith, "is a willingness to put his personal life and affairs into the hands of Jesus Christ – without qualification and without reservation." This is what Christ refers to when He talks about taking up the cross daily. It means being prepared day by day to put self-interest to death and to say, "No longer my will, but yours be done."

Matthew 26:36–46

When the urge towards self-assertion, self-aggrandisement and self-pleasing gives way to the desire to please God, much of the strain goes out of life. Dr William Sadler, the psychiatrist, tells of a lady he once treated who said to him, "You know, I am a very sensitive person." "Yes," said Dr Sadler, "I know you are a very selfish person." "But I didn't say 'selfish'", protested the woman. "I did", replied the doctor. She went away angry but ten days later came back, chastened, and confessed it was true. Her self-centredness was the basis of her illness.

The Man who was the healthiest person that ever lived on our planet, a Man who radiated health – only to touch Him was to be made whole – followed the way of His Father right to the very end. When confronted by the Cross, He was greatly tempted to follow His own desires and take the way that seemed best to Him, but came through the struggle to say: "Father … not as I will, but as you will." God's way is not just a way, or even the best way – it is the Way.

The reward of following the Lord's path, rather than our own self-determined ways, is that we shall be led from one good pasture to another.

An efficient shepherd always tries to keep his sheep on the move, thus avoiding over-use of the land and enabling his sheep to continually enjoy wholesome, fresh forage.

Phillip Keller says, in commenting on this point: "… whenever the shepherd opens a gate into fresh pasture, the sheep are filled with excitement. As they go through the gate even the staid old ewes will often kick up their heels and leap with delight at the prospect of finding fresh feed. How they enjoy being led on to new ground."

Do you experience a similar delight as the Good Shepherd leads you day by day to wholesome, fresh forage? Are you one of those Christians who want to continually feed on just one doctrine or truth, and never go on to enjoy the other delights which God has for you in His Word? Be assured of this – God wants us to move with Him day by day to discover new insights and fresh revelation as He opens up to us the glories of His precious Word. Every Christian should meet the day with as much delight as a sheep that is being led into fresh new pasture. Spiritually, we should kick up our heels and leap with delight at the prospect of finding fresh new forage. Expect God to show you some new insight day by day. Faith is expectancy – according to your expectancy be it unto you.

John 16:1–15

The valley of
the shadow of death

We come now to the phrase which many commentators see as marking the halfway stage of this psalm: "Even though I walk through the valley of the shadow of death, I will fear no evil, for you are with me". The scene that these words conjure up in our minds is that of evening time, when the shepherd leads his sheep down the mountainside into the valley, where flickering shadows lie across the trail. The sheep, because they are so timid and defenceless, are usually frightened by this experience. But they follow the shepherd and therefore are comforted. They will not fear evil because the shepherd is with them.

Millions of Christians have been greatly comforted by this verse as they have passed through the dark valley of death. It underlines the fact that although death may be a dark valley, it is not something to fear, but an experience through which one passes on the path to a more perfect life. The Good Shepherd is well aware of our fear of death and constantly seeks to reassure us that, for the Christian, death is but a dark valley opening out into an eternity of endless delight. He has told us: "Surely I will be with you always – yes, even in the valley of the shadow of death." What a comfort – what a consolation.

Many Christians fail to enjoy life because of a morbid fear of death – it overshadows all they think and do. Look at how Moffatt translates Hebrews 2:15: "And release from thraldom those who lay under a life-long fear of death". Note the terror in some of the words: "thraldom", "lay under", "life-long fear of death". Can there be a release from such fears? Thank God – there can!

Hebrews 2:5–18

Many people, some Christians included, see death as an intruder. Gandhi, the great Indian leader and politician, said that he started his Swaraj movement to help people overcome the fear of death. Politics was only a minor part of his purpose. "My aim", he said, "was the abandonment of the fear of death. So long as we let ourselves be influenced by the fear of death, we can never attain freedom."

When we come to analyse the fear of death, three elements can be seen to be present. First, the fear of the physical act of dying. Secondly, the fear of finality. Thirdly, the fear of judgment. Let's look first at the fear of the physical act of dying. This is very real to some people. Perhaps they have suffered and know, through bitter experience, how pain lacerates and hurts.

Isaiah 43:1–13

Doctors assure us that what people normally call "the agony of death" is felt much more by those who are watching than by the one who is passing away. Sir Frederick Treves, the eminent surgeon, said, "A last illness may be long, wearisome and painful, but the closing moments of it are, as a rule, free from suffering. There may appear to be a terrible struggle at the end, but of this struggle the subject is unconscious. It is the onlooker who bears the misery of it." Add to this natural phenomenon the supporting power of God's never-failing grace, and it is possible to look even this physical aspect of death quietly in the face and say, "My enemy – you are not really the terror that you seem."

Then there is the fear of finality. No Christian need fear that death is equivalent to extinction, for Christ has said: "I go to prepare a place for you … that where I am you may be also" (John 14:2–3, RSV). Dr W.E. Sangster tells how, as a young boy living in the heart of London, he went for a walk one day and got lost. A kindly policeman took him by the hand and led him to the police station. After waiting for what seemed like several hours in a dingy room, a stern officer came and took him down a dark passage where he saw his father waiting for him. Sangster said, "It will not be different, I think, when I die. At the end of the dark passage my Father will be waiting." Though we shrink in the frail of our human nature from what some refer to as "the Grim Reaper", death really has but one mission – to bring us into God's more immediate presence and give us an eternal place in our Father's house.

John 14:1–14

Finally, let us take the fear of judgment. Some research conducted a few years ago showed that this third component is not as common as it was. Fewer people now attend church, and those who do, generally speaking, rarely hear a sermon on the fact of future judgment. No man or woman, however, who knows Christ should fear judgment. And why? Because, as Paul so beautifully puts it in his letter to the Romans: "Therefore, there is now no condemnation for those who are in Christ Jesus". In Christ, judgment is in the past tense.

Earth's gloom
to heaven's glory

The whole teaching of Scripture, and particularly the words of Christ concerning life after death, deepens Christian confidence. We delight in the words, "I go to prepare a place for you", but He said something that surpasses even this: "In My Father's house are many dwelling places; if it were not so, I would have told you" (John 14:2, NASB).

Acts 7:54–60

Jesus says, in effect: "If seventy years of life, more or less, were all that you could expect, I would be open with you and encourage you to make the most of the time you spend on this earth ... but in my Father's house ..." Take again the way Jesus and the New Testament use the words "death" and "sleep". To the mourners standing around the lifeless body of a little girl, Jesus said: "The child is not dead but asleep" (Mark 5:39). He used the same word also when talking of the death of Lazarus: "Our friend Lazarus has fallen asleep; but I am going there to wake him up" (John 11:11).

Although I haven't checked his statement, one commentator makes the daring assertion that in the New Testament, after Jesus' death and resurrection, no one who was a Christian was ever said to have died. He claims that when sin had done its utmost in nailing Christ to the tree and hiding His tortured body in a sepulchre sealed by a huge stone, it was still powerless to destroy the Life which used His flesh. Death was dead – not He! Now everything "in Christ" is alive, and thus the vocabulary has to be changed to fit the facts. What we call "death", and Jesus called "falling asleep", is simply the transition from one plane of life to another – from earth's gloom to heaven's glory.

The Christian faith is the only faith that lights up that dark area of human existence – death. "And it lights it up," says Stanley E. Jones, "not merely with a word but with a Word become flesh." Jesus went through the dark experience we call death, and the word of resurrection became flesh in Him. Anyone who lives in Him is as deathless as He is deathless.

1 Corinthians 15:42–57

It was said of Emerson, the great writer and debater: "He did not argue; he let in the light." The same can also be said of Jesus: "He did not argue immortality, He showed Himself alive." The greatest evidence for the fact that there is life after death is, as we said, the resurrection of Jesus Christ. One of Tennyson's biographers wrote: "He laid his mind upon the minds of others with the result that they believed his beliefs." Well, Jesus does the same. He lays His mind upon ours and we believe His beliefs. He not only believed in immortality, but demonstrated it. I believe in it, too – and so, I hope, do you. His living guarantees our living.

A woman was teaching a group of Japanese children on the island of Hawaii about the life and death of Jesus, when one of the children jumped out into the aisle and cried out: "Ah … this no fair … Him one swell guy." One little girl who knew the story pulled him by the coat tails and urged him to sit down. "Don't get upset", she said. "He didn't stay dead." Well, if He didn't stay dead, nor shall I stay dead. William James, when asked if he believed in personal immortality, said: "Yes — and the more strongly as I grow older. Why? Because I'm just getting fit to live." I, too, am just getting fit to live. How about you?

No discipline
– no disciples

Having seen something of how the words, "Even though I walk through the valley of the shadow of death", relate to us as Christians, we move on now to consider the phrase: "... your rod and your staff, they comfort me."

Shepherds, in Bible days, carried very little equipment with them when they tended their sheep, but invariably they carried a rod and a staff. The rod was a club which was used for a number of purposes, but mainly to drive off wild animals or catch the sheep's attention. If a shepherd saw a sheep wandering from the path or approaching a potentially dangerous situation – such as poisonous weeds, or the edge of a precipice – he would hurl his rod slightly ahead of the sheep, thus startling it for a moment and causing it to scurry back to the safety of the flock.

The rod therefore became an object of discipline, not to hurt or injure the sheep, but to direct it back into the way. Young shepherds would train for hours and compete with each other to see who could throw his rod with the greatest accuracy and across the greatest distance. The rod was what a shepherd relied on to protect both himself and his sheep whenever there was the threat of danger.

Deuteronomy 8:1–18

How many of us, I wonder, can go through the Christian life day after day without the need for some discipline? I can't – and I'm sure that is true of you also. Someone described the Christian life in this way: "Dependence plus discipline equals dependable disciples." Notice – dependence plus discipline … You can't be a dependable disciple without discipline No discipline – no disciple. It's as simple as that!

"Discipline's divine design"

Observing the way in which a shepherd in Bible days used his rod to discipline his sheep and bring them back into the way gives us a glimpse into the character of God. Some Christians have such a distorted view of God that they interpret His disciplines as punishment, and fail to see that the reason why our heavenly Father disciplines us is not because He is angry with us, but because He loves us.

1 Timothy
1:1–17

To understand God's purpose in disciplining us, it is necessary to observe the difference between two things – fear and respect. The Bible uses the word "fear" in two ways: (1) as a form of anxiety, and (2) as a form of respect. As Christians, it is right that we have a deep respect for the Almighty, but we must see also that God does not want us to live out our days in anxiety, apprehension and dread.

Some parents attempt to influence and discipline their children through the use of anxiety and apprehension, but God does not deal with His children on that basis. One woman I heard of, wanting to teach her daughter the rules of the road, took her down to a busy crossroads and shouted to her as the cars approached: "Look out – here comes a car!" The child soon learned how to keep out of the way of approaching cars, but she also developed a morbid fear of traffic. One of the goals of parenthood is to so train children that they develop respect without fear. 1 Timothy 1:5 says: "The goal of this command is love, which comes from a pure heart …" The aim of God's discipline is not fear – but love that springs – and sings!

Rarely should we use the word "punishment" in relation to the disciplines which God effects in our lives as Christians. Although there is a sense in which God is bound to punish sin, in the life of Christian as well as a non-Christian, the thought uppermost in God's mind when disciplining a Christian is not retribution for past misdeeds, but the development of future maturity. Bruce Narramore, a Christian psychologist, believes that the word "punishment" should be reserved for non-Christians only. He says, speaking of the relationship that God has with His children, that "as Christ took our punishment on the Cross, we are no longer sinners, but saints. Thereafter the focus of God's dealings with us is not retributive, but remedial. We Christians are not under punishment, but under discipline – and the difference is vital."

Proverbs 3:1–12

I find it difficult to believe myself that God's disciplines do not contain an element of punishment, but I see the point Bruce Narramore is making – namely, that when we do wrong or wander from the pathway, God does not pounce upon us so as to even the score; His disciplines follow a divine design that is calculated, not merely to punish our wrongdoing, but to promote our spiritual growth and maturity. How consoling this thought is – that when we disobey, God intervenes to correct us, not in anger, or with a desire to get even with us, but out of the deepest concern and interest for our spiritual development and well-being.

Hand in hand

Having seen that the main purpose of a shepherd's rod was to lovingly discipline his sheep, we turn now to consider the next item of his equipment – the staff. "It is the staff", says Phillip Keller, "that identifies a shepherd as a shepherd. No one in any other profession carries a shepherd's staff. It is uniquely an instrument used for the care and management of sheep. It will not do for cattle, horses or hogs. It is designed, shaped and adapted especially to the needs of sheep."

The staff was a slender pole with a little crook on the end, and was used for a variety of purposes. It was used to gently lift a newborn lamb and bring it to its mother when it had become separated, (A ewe will sometimes reject her offspring if it has the smell of human hands upon it.) It was used also to reach out and draw a sheep to the shepherd's side for physical examination, as timid and nervous sheep tend to keep as much distance as possible between themselves and the shepherd.

The main use of an ancient shepherd's staff, however, was to guide the sheep. The tip of the staff would be laid against the animal's side, and the gentle pressure applied would guide the sheep in the way the shepherd wanted it to go. One observer of the ways of a shepherd with his sheep says, "Sometimes I have been fascinated to see how a shepherd will actually hold his staff against the side of a nervous or frightened sheep simply so that they are 'in touch'. They will walk along the way almost as though they were hand in hand. To be treated in this special way by the shepherd is to know comfort in a deep dimension."

Isaiah 51:1–16

I hesitated to use the shepherd's staff as a type of the Holy Spirit, but as I considered the caring and comforting ministry of the Good Shepherd, my mind ran immediately to John 14. Listen to what Jesus said in verse 16: "And I will pray the Father, and he shall give you another Comforter, that he may abide with you for ever"(AV). Notice that Jesus used the pronoun "He", indicating that the Holy Spirit is not an influence, but a person. He is a person who counsels, comforts, guides, empowers – but most of all abides. An impersonal influence – an "It" – doesn't do that!

Modern translations substitute for the word "Comforter" such words as "Helper", "Counsellor" or "Strengthener". But the Greek word is *parakaleo*: *para*, meaning "beside", *kaleo*, meaning "to call" – one who is called alongside us. Why is He called alongside? For counsel? Yes. For strength? Yes. For everything? Yes. There isn't a single thing needed for life that He isn't there to provide. Just as a shepherd walks alongside his sheep to comfort and to guide, so the Holy Spirit has come among us to bring the reality of Christ's word and presence to our hearts. It is through Him that we are in touch with Christ, and it is through Him also that there steals over us the assurance that we are one with Him and that we "belong". Oh, the security of being under His constant supervision and care. Too good to be true? Too good not to be true.

"He has gone ahead"

A s we turn to focus on the next phrase in the "Shepherd Psalm", we cannot help but notice that David appears to change the metaphor – from the good shepherd to the gracious host: "You prepare a table before me in the presence of my enemies".

Isaiah 25:1–9

Many commentators take this as a natural division in the psalm, and thus claim that it is written in two parts: the first using the figure of a shepherd and his sheep, and the second using the figure of a banquet with the host and the guest. One writer says: "It's a pity that David didn't finish his psalm by staying with the one figure of a shepherd, rather than bringing in the concept of a banquet and a host. It seems to me to lose the sweet simple melody and to close with strange heavy chords when it changes to a scene of banquet hospitality."

That conclusion is quite wrong, for despite the seeming change of metaphor, David actually keeps the shepherd figure right to the end. When David referred to a "table", he was not thinking of an indoor banquet, but of the high, flat-topped plateaus where the sheep were taken to graze in the summertime. Prior to taking his sheep on to this higher ground, a caring and concerned shepherd would go up alone to see if there were any wild animals or any poisonous weeds and, if so, plan his grazing programme to either avoid them or take whatever steps were necessary to eradicate them. The sheep arriving on the high tableland would not, of course, realise it, but they owed their safety and security to the fact that the shepherd had gone before them to prepare for them a "table" in the presence of their enemies.

Those who have studied ancient Bible customs and the ways of eastern shepherds state, quite categorically: "There is no higher task for a shepherd than to go from time to time to study places, examine the grass and find a good and safe feeding place for his sheep." There are many poisonous plants in the grass and the shepherd must find them and avoid them. It has been known for a shepherd to lose hundreds of sheep in one day by failing to take the necessary precautions in this matter.

Another observer of eastern customs says: "There are vipers' holes from which the poisonous snakes emerge to bite the noses of the sheep. The shepherd must burn the fat of hogs at the holes to bring out the snakes and then either kill them or drive them away." In addition to these dangers around the feeding ground, there are holes and caves in the hillside in which live wolves and jackals. The bravery and heroism of the shepherd reaches its highest point as he works to close up these dens with stones, or

confront and kill the beasts with his long-bladed knife. Of
nothing did the ancient shepherds boast more proudly
than of their achievements in securing a safe feeding
ground for their flocks.

The way God protects and cares for His children as
they go out into the world is a grander and more
wonderful thought than that of seating them at an indoor
banqueting table. If it is not apparent already, it should be
quite clear by now that in those quaint and beautiful lines
"You prepare a table before me in the presence of my
enemies", the shepherd figure is as real as in the previous
section of the psalm.

1 Peter 1:1–9

Staying close
to the Shepherd

A classic example of the way in which the divine Shepherd ministers to His children is seen in Luke 22. Jesus tells Simon Peter that Satan has sought to tempt him and sift him like wheat, but that He has prayed that Peter's faith might not fail in that moment of overwhelming testing. Where would I have been, where would you have been, but for that blessed ministry of the divine Shepherd – going before us, anticipating our circumstances and supportively working and praying for us, so that we might not be overtaken by the enemy of our souls? If He did not minister to us in this way … where should we be?

Luke 22:24–33

This does not mean, of course, that the responsibility for our safety and security rests entirely on our divine Shepherd. We, too, have a responsibility – a responsibility to make sure that we keep as close to Him as we possibly can. This is the one sure place of safety. "It is always the distant sheep, the roamers, the wanderers," says one shepherd, "which are picked off by predators in an unsuspecting moment. Sometimes the sheep is so overtaken by fear that it is too frightened to even cry out. It might give a plaintive bleat before its blood is spilled." The divine Shepherd wants to forestall every calamity that would come our way, and strives to keep our lives free from serious dangers and hazards. And, of course, our lives will be danger free if we stay close to Him, where He can provide for us and protect us.

The object
of His love

Some commentators believe that when David wrote the words, "You prepare a table before me in the presence of my enemies", he had in mind the events about which we read in 2 Samuel 17. Driven into the wilderness by his son Absalom's rebellion, David and his followers became desperately hungry, thirsty and weary. God came to his aid, however and directed to him three men – Shobi, Makir and Barzillai – who "brought bedding and bowls" (so that David could wash and refresh himself) as well as "articles of pottery … wheat and barley, flour and roasted grain, beans and lentils, honey and curds, sheep, and cheese …".

2 Samuel
17:20–29

How David must have rubbed his eyes in astonishment as he saw God provide for him a "table in the presence of his enemies". Can you cast your mind back at this moment to something "special" that God did for you to demonstrate His tender love and care? I can. Every Christian has these times – how sad that we forget them so soon.

You see, God never does anything "special" in our lives just for the sake of the passing hour – it is done also as a pledge for the future. It is as though God is saying: "I'll do this for you now, not only to meet your need, but that you might always know you are the object of my love." And I say again – what a tragedy that we forget so soon. That is why new dangers startle us with fear and dismay. We have forgotten the past mercies. I don't doubt myself that David's calmness and confidence in God was due, in no small measure, to the fact that whenever he faced a new problem, he remembered vividly the past hour of deliverance.

A shepherd, more often than not, has to go through a good deal of personal sacrifice and danger in order to prepare the "table", or feeding ground, for his sheep. He may have to endure loneliness, privation, hunger and sometimes even physical injury in his efforts to make the feeding ground safe for his sheep. Many a shepherd comes back from such an expedition covered in cuts and bruises.

Just as a good shepherd sacrifices himself for the sake of his sheep, so has Christ, the Good Shepherd, gone to the utmost lengths possible to bring His sheep into a place of spiritual contentment and security. Unfortunately we forget all too easily just what was the personal cost to Christ in preparing the table for His redeemed people. When next you come to the Table of Communion – which is really a feast of thanksgiving in remembrance of His tender love and care – ask yourself: do I fully appreciate what it cost my Lord to prepare this table for me? And what did it cost? It cost Him His life.

As Christmas Evans, one of our great Welsh preachers, picturesquely put it: "Never did any shepherd climb a mountain as dangerous and as challenging as Mount Calvary. There on its summit the Good Shepherd drew sin to battle, overcame all its forces, silenced forever the voice of the archenemy of our souls – and by so doing has prepared for us a table in the presence of our enemies. Come and be fed …"

1 John 3:11–24

Those stupid flies!

We turn to focus on the next phrase in this beautiful and inspired psalm: "You anoint my head with oil; my cup overflows". To understand the meaning of this delightful statement we must once again draw on the experience of those who have spent their lives keeping sheep, and know from firsthand experience the problems of these peculiar but fascinating animals.

Sheep, we are told, are especially irritated by flies and other winged parasites which buzz around their heads and make their lives a misery. *The Handbook of Bible Times and Customs* lists over twenty varieties of flies that can be found in the Middle East – warble flies, deer flies, black flies, nose flies and so on. "Sheep are especially troubled by nose flies," says one shepherd, "for they buzz around the head of a sheep attempting to alight on the damp mucous membranes of the sheep's nose." So irritating can be the effect of nose flies that sometimes a sheep will beat its head against a tree or a rock in order to find relief. An alert shepherd, when he sees this taking place, goes to the sheep that is in trouble and bathes its head in olive oil. This results, almost immediately, in a dramatic change in the sheep's behaviour. Gone is the frenzy and restlessness and soon the sheep begins to quietly graze or lie down in peaceful contentment.

Perhaps at this very moment you are facing an endless bombardment of irritations and difficulties that are causing you to become downcast and fainthearted. Draw near to Jesus – your heavenly Shepherd. Spend some moments in quite prayer and contemplation. Let Him bathe your hurts in the soothing oil of the Spirit. Then rise and go your way in the knowledge that no matter how frustrating life's   Ezekiel 34:1–16 circumstances and situations the divine Shepherd is only a prayer away.

When evil
thoughts molest

We saw that relief from flies and other winged parasites buzzing around the head of a sheep comes only when the shepherd is able to bathe the sheep's head with the soothing oil which he carries with him for this purpose. What a striking picture this presents of the way in which God ministers to us in the midst of life's irritations. A motto on the desk of a high school principal reads:

For every irritation under the sun
There is a remedy, or there is none
If there be one, try to find it,
If there be none, never mind it.

The suggestion, regarding an irritation for which there is no remedy, to "never mind it" is good, but not quite good enough. The irritation may be so present and insistent that you cannot help but mind it.

Take, for example, the evil or lustful thoughts that sometimes buzz around in our heads. It is impossible not to mind them. What is to be done? Several things are possible. First build a strong picture of Christ in your mind. In your reading, meditation, and personal prayer time, seek to develop a clear picture of your Saviour. Then, when a wrong thought strikes, focus your mind, not on the thought, but on Him. Wrong thoughts can be outwitted by swiftly directing the mind to a more

absorbing theme. And what better theme is there in the whole realm of thought than Christ?

Isaiah 26:1–12

The minute a wrong or obsessive thought comes into the mind and is recognised, we should look immediately to the Lord. Our victory depends on the skill we develop in quickly turning from the wrong thought to focus on Christ.

Philippians 4:1–9

A second way in which some Christians have learned how to outwit the power of evil thoughts is not only to fix their minds on Jesus, but to use also, as lesser helps, any wholesome subject in which they have a keen interest. A university graduate tells how, once he realised that the battle against evil thoughts had to be won where it had begun – in the mind – he could quickly shut off a train of wrong thoughts by anticipating the graduation ceremony at which he hoped to receive his degree. He said he focused also on other wholesome things – such as his hobbies, or an intriguing sermon he had heard – and he proved by experience that with practice and determination he could divert his mind into interesting and clean channels.

As you can see, much of the success in overcoming wrong thoughts depends on how one prepares for the conflict – for conflict it is. When Paul encourages us to reflect upon things which are true, noble, right, pure, lovely and admirable, he is giving us good advice. To think and keep on thinking of these things, with a picture of Jesus at the centre of them, is the only adequate preparation for the fight against evil thoughts. The supreme Helper is Christ.

John 16:16–33

When evil thoughts molest,
With this I shield my breast –
May Jesus Christ be praised!

We must not only focus our gaze upon Christ when worn down by the thoughts that buzz around inside our heads, but we must come to Him in petitionary prayer and ask Him to help us. In talking over the years with people who were plagued with evil thoughts, I have been surprised at the number who have told me that they have never actually come to God and asked directly for His help. James reminds us that one of the reasons why we do not receive is simply because we do not ask (James 4:2).

How, then, do we ask? It can be done in your own words or in the words of an appropriate hymn. You can say something like this: "Father, lay Your consoling hand on this forehead which is oppressed with irritating and evil thoughts. Help me now by breaking their hold upon me, and release me from their grip. In Jesus' Name." It must be understood, of course, that as well as praying, you, too, must accept some responsibility in this matter. It's no good praying, "Lord, deliver me from this evil thought", and then wallowing in it in your imagination. God will do His part, but you must also do yours.

Today we ask ourselves: just how does our Lord go about the task of responding to our petitions to be delivered from wrong or distracting thoughts? He does it through the gentle, yet powerful ministry of the Holy Spirit.

The words "oil" and "anoint" are used in Scripture to depict several things, not the least being comfort, gladness and consolation (Psa. 45:7). It is this thought, of course, which the psalmist had in mind when he wrote, "You anoint my head with oil; my cup overflows". When a Christian is driven almost to distraction by the obsessive or evil thoughts that buzz around in his head, the most important thing he can do is to approach the Shepherd and say: "O Lord, help me – apply the soothing oil of Your Spirit to every area of my mind." And you know what? He will! It will surprise you how speedily and efficiently He complies with such a request when it is made in deadly earnest.

Some Christians make it their daily petition to ask God for the anointing of the Spirit upon their minds. Coolness in place of heat, and peace instead of torment are the rewards of those who are swift to turn to the Shepherd and invite Him to minister to them in this way. So when thoughts seem to niggle you and almost drive you up the wall, draw close to the Shepherd and let Him apply the oil of the Spirit to your troubled and anxious mind. And you need have no fears that His supply of oil is limited in any way. He draws from a cup that never runs dry: "You anoint my head with oil; my cup overflows".

Psalm 19:12–14

The Hound
of Heaven

Whe move on now to consider the phrase: "Surely goodness and mercy shall follow me all the days of my life"(AV). Even the most casual reader cannot help but be struck with the fact that, throughout this psalm, David has placed a continuous emphasis on the care and diligence of the divine Shepherd. He has made it abundantly clear that all the benefits enjoyed by the believer are due in no small measure to the skill and management of the Good Shepherd. With such a Shepherd, we need never fear, for no matter what difficulties and problems we may encounter, He follows hard on our heels to redeem every single event and situation.

Luke 15:1–7

The word "follow" in this phrase literally means "pursue" – thus it could just as well be translated: "Goodness and mercy shall pursue me all the days of my life". David is saying that although his enemies are pursuing him to dethrone and destroy him, God is

following even harder on his heels to dispense the twin qualities of goodness and mercy. Francis Thompson in his memorable poem entitled *The Hound of Heaven*, put the same thought in this way:

> ... *those strong Feet that followed, followed after.*
> *But with unhurrying chase*
> *And unperturbed pace*
> *Deliberate speed, majestic instancy*
> *They beat – and a Voice beat*
> *More instant than the Feet –*
> *"All things betray thee, who betrayest Me."*

Many consider that when David uttered the phrase he was simply being poetic and not proclaiming a solid fact. They say: "It's easy to repeat this statement and believe it when everything is going well, but what about those times when health fails, or income falls and troubles 'come not single spies, but in battalions'?" And what about those times also when we have to watch a loved one writhe in the agonies of unrelieved pain, or when close friends prove false and disloyal? Can we really say at such times: "Surely goodness and mercy shall follow me all the days of my life ..."?

Philippians
1:12–30

I believe we can.

As I look back over my life, I can remember many events and circumstances which I viewed at the time as calamities. I can recollect one particular occasion – during 1968 – when, as I looked forward into the future, things looked so black that I considered leaving the ministry. Now, with hindsight, I can see that the hour of darkness was one of the great turning-points in my life, and moved me, not toward a lesser ministry, but a wider one. Goodness and mercy followed me, and turned what looked like despair into a door of greater opportunity.

It is my belief that God does not engineer what we might describe as "calamities" or "disasters", but that they happen as the consequence of sin, ignorance or carelessness. Such is His skill, however, at turning tragedy to triumph and loss into gain that I can understand why some believe He sent the tragedy and devised the disaster – so marvellously does He bring good out of evil.

Many people saw the loss of the *Titanic* in 1912 as an act of God's judgment because of the proud boast of its owners that it was "unsinkable". I do not see it in that light at all. The loss of the *Titanic* was due to reckless racing through an icefield, and the death toll was greater than it needed to have been by reason of the fact that she only carried lifeboat accommodation for 1,200 people, though the passengers and crew totalled 2,293. The great ship went down due to a compound of pride and criminal folly. "Many a life," says one writer, "has been saved by the *Titanic*. The track of westbound ships across the Atlantic was shifted further south, away from the dangerous ice-fields. The obsolete Board of Trade requirements with regard to emergency boat accommodation were stringently revised."

This is often the way it is in life – disappointment, tragedy and grief teach people a great deal. In the Christian life, however, this is not often the way it is – but always the way it is. God follows hard on the heels of every event and circumstance in our lives, not only teaching us a great deal, but working to turn every loss into a gain. Look back over your life for a moment. Have there not been times when you questioned God's wisdom and management of your affairs? Have you not had moments when you thought you could survive better on your own? But what is your view now? Are you not convinced that He followed you in goodness and mercy? Did not good come out of the evil, light out of darkness, and faith out of despair?

Isaiah 41:1–16

What a difference!

I t probably goes without saying that this phrase of
David's – "Surely goodness and mercy shall follow me
all the days of my life"(AV) – is an utterance of faith.
It can be said only by someone who looks beyond the
events and circumstances of life and has implicit
confidence in the One who is ultimately in control. David
believed that nothing could happen to him, no difficulty
or dilemma could come into his life without eventual
good emerging from the chaos. Most of us, when we look
back in our lives, can see the truth of this, but the
challenge is to believe it when we are going through the
circumstances. Ah, then it is not so easy.

James 1:2–18

Have you ever heard of Phillip Brooks? He was one of
the great preachers of a previous generation. He began his
career as a schoolteacher and both he and his advisors had
every reason to believe that he would do well. But he was
a failure. He went home to his parents mortified beyond
words. In the midst of his depression, there came to him a
clear call to the Christian ministry. At first he pushed it
aside, but the call grew louder and louder. He was led on
step by step to become a preacher of amazing influence,
gaining a position of high esteem on both sides of the
Atlantic.

He says in one of his sermons on the 23rd Psalm: "In
the hours of my humiliation, if anyone had said to me that
'God's goodness and mercy' were following hard on my
heels, I would have considered them an imbecile. But they
did! How differently I might have responded if I had
believed then, as I believe now, that His goodness and

mercy are my constant companions." How differently indeed!

The thought which has been quietly shaping itself in our minds is a powerful and transforming one – namely, that the goodness and mercy of God follow hard on our heels to turn every tragedy into a triumph and every loss into a gain. It is easy to affirm this as we look back – the challenge is to affirm it with equal conviction as we look ahead.

Acts 13:13–31

If you can get hold of this truth and absorb it into your life as a working principle, then it will transform your attitude to everything. Never again will you be at the mercy of circumstances. In Acts 5:40–41 we read an astonishing statement: "When they had called in the apostles, they beat them … Then they left the presence of the council, rejoicing …" (RSV). Rejoicing? Over injustice? How is it possible to rejoice over an injustice? Because they believed, with David, that the last word was not with men, but with God – "goodness and mercy" would follow them and turn the situation to their advantage. When you can rejoice over injustice, you are indomitable.

Another verse from Acts that always intrigues me reads thus: "Because the patriarchs were jealous of Joseph, they sold him as a slave into Egypt. But God …" (Acts 7:9). That phrase, "but God", is at the end of every injustice – He has the last word. And just as God used the injustice done to Joseph to feed the Egyptian people and his own family, so He transforms every injustice, every sorrow, every bereavement, every tragedy. Christianity may not explain everything, but it most certainly transforms everything.

"I'll never
leave this outfit!"

W e come now to the final phrase in David's "hymn of praise to divine diligence": "I will dwell in the house of the Lord for ever". We said when we began our meditations on this psalm – and the point has been repeatedly emphasised throughout – that David is not speaking here as a shepherd, though he was one, but as a sheep; one of God's flock.

Psalm 84:1–12

David knew, better than anyone, that a sheep's welfare depended to a great degree on the love and care of its shepherd. Having begun with the proud boast, "The Lord is my shepherd" – or, as someone translates it, "Look at who my shepherd is – my owner, my manager – the Lord is!" – he finishes on an equally positive note: "I will dwell in the house of the Lord for ever". The thought that comes through in this final phrase is clearly this – I am so utterly contented with being under the care of my loving Shepherd that I have no wish to have my circumstances changed – I want things to stay this way for ever!

Some commentators have expressed disappointment at David's use of the word "house" in the closing phrase of his psalm, believing it to detract somewhat from the imagery of a shepherd and his sheep. But the word "house" has a much wider meaning than most seem to attach to it. It means, in fact, the "household" of God, the "flock" of God – or, as the Amplified Bible translates it – the "presence" of God. Phillip Keller's rugged translation of this final phrase may offend the purists, but to me it states fairly accurately what was in the psalmist's mind. "Nothing will ever make me leave this outfit! It's great!" And to that I add a hearty Amen!

As one of the sheep of God's flock, David is so satisfied with the care and management of his Shepherd that he wants things to stay that way – for ever. He has no wish or desire to change, and his words ring with positive assurance: "I will dwell in the house of the Lord for ever".

A Harvard University professor once lectured on the theme: "Is eternal existence desirable?" and came to the conclusion that it is not. If all that eternity offers is just existence, then I would tend to agree with the professor's conclusion. Who can bear mere existence eternally? But if it's eternal life – that's different. "Life has to be eternal or else it is not worth living."

John 17:1–19

Dr E. Stanley Jones, when referring to the subject of life after death, remarked: "Only life that is eternal is really life: every other kind of life has the seeds of death in it." George Bernard Shaw once said, "I don't want to have to live with George Bernard Shaw for ever." We can hardly blame some people for not wanting to live with themselves for ever, because they are poor companions to themselves now. A lot of people dislike themselves, and thus to spend eternity with a self you dislike is not a happy prospect. But suppose you have a self that is transformed into the image of Christ – and not only changed into His image, but joined to Him inseparably – what then? Ah – that is different! That is more than existence – that is life. Remember, eternity is not just living for ever – it is living with Jesus for ever. That's what makes the difference.

"An assurance was given me"

avid feels so safe and secure in the flock of God that he has no hesitation in affirming that this is the way it will be for ever. Do you, I wonder, feel as safe and secure in your Christian life as David did in the Shepherd's fold?

This is not the time or place to debate the issue of "eternal security" – or, as it is sometimes described, "once saved, always saved" – but it is right to focus here on that most blessed of all earthly experiences – assurance. The question is often raised in Christian circles: can a person have, in this life, the assurance of personal salvation? One denomination gives this answer: "It is not possible to know in this life, with any degree of certainty, that one is a recipient of the grace of God."

Romans 8:1–17

What utter nonsense! Listen again to those now famous words which John Wesley wrote in his journal after going "very reluctantly" to a room in Aldersgate Street, London, on May 24th 1738, where a reading was being given from Luther's Preface to the Book of Romans: "I felt my heart strangely warmed. I felt I did trust in Christ, Christ alone, for salvation, and an assurance was given me that He had taken away my sins, even mine, and saved me from the law of sin and death." An assurance was given me! Wesley had the assurance of salvation. And so, I might humbly add, do I. But what is more important, as far as you are concerned, is that if you surrender your life fully to Jesus Christ and trust Him alone for your soul's salvation, then so can you.

One section of the Christian Church affirms that it is not possible for a person to know with a certainty of faith that is not liable to illusion that he or she is a recipient of God's grace. Another section of the Church says that to affirm one is "saved" savours of presumption and spiritual pride. They say: "We can state that we hope to be saved, or that we are trying to be saved, or that we are being saved, but no one can say, 'I am saved', until he arrives safely over on the other side."

Ian MacPherson, in his book *This Man Loved Me*, tells how one day a woman came to him and said, "I think it is great presumption for a person to say they are saved." He asked her if she was saved. "I belong to a church", she said. "But are you saved?" he continued. She replied: "But I believe it would be presumption for me to say that I am saved." "Well," said the preacher, "I think it is greater presumption for anyone professing to believe in Jesus not to say that he is saved – for Christ Himself declares: 'He who believes in Me has everlasting life.'"

The Bible makes it clear that we cannot only be

assured of salvation in this life, and certain that when we die we will go straight into the immediate presence of the Lord, but that we can be fully assured that we have eternal life – as our text for today makes clear. An old Welsh miner who used to write to me many years ago used to put after his name the letters MA. I knew he did not have a Master's degree and I asked him what it meant. "Oh," he said, "it's simple. It means that in relation to being with Christ in eternity, I am Mightily Assured."

John 6:35–51

Christians – that is, true Christians – not only have an assurance that when they die they will go to heaven, but they also have a nostalgia for it. The word "nostalgia" comes from two Greek words: "*nostos*", meaning "return home"; and "*algos*", meaning "pain". It meant, originally, incurable homesickness – incurable by anything, except, of course, by home.

2 Corinthians 5:1–15

An old legend of the Western Isles tells of a seal king who desired the company of a human being. One day he heard, from his cavern under the sea, a baby's cry – and he rose to the surface to discover a tiny infant in a derelict boat. Just as he was about to make for the vessel, a rescue party intervened – and he lost his prize. But – so the legend goes – as the boat was towed away, the seal king threw into the heart of the child a little salt wave, saying as he submerged, "The child is mine. When he grows, the salt sea will call him and he will come home."

It is only a legend, of course, but it underlines the timeless truth that when God comes into our lives we have not only the assurance that we belong to Him, but a deep, insatiable longing for Home. One preacher claims there are two things you notice about a Christian who is head over heels in love with Christ. You notice first how natural and "at home" he is, and the next thing you say to yourself is, "This man is an exile; he doesn't belong here at all." You can observe this in the apostle Paul. How busy and concerned he was for Christ's affairs on earth, and yet he sighs, as in 2 Corinthians 5:8, to be "at home with the Lord". Do you have a nostalgia for heaven?

No separation
– for ever

We come now to the end of our meditations on the sublime phrases of what someone has described as "the sweetest religious song ever written – the twenty-third Psalm". It began with a positive note of assurance: "The Lord is my shepherd, I shall not want"(AV), and it ends in the same joyous and exhilarating way: "I will dwell in the house of the Lord for ever".

This Psalm, as we have seen, pictures a sheep so fully satisfied, so utterly content and so much "at home" with the shepherd that there is not the slightest desire for change. Conversely, of course, on the shepherd's side, such a relationship has developed that he would never think of parting with one of his sheep. So strong are the bonds between them that nothing can separate them – ever.

John 10:22–38

As I conclude, there comes to mind a memory from the days when I first entered the ministry in the lovely farming county of Carmarthenshire in West Wales. Many of the farmers in the area were deeply caring of their sheep, but there was one who was notorious for his disinterest and neglect. When one looked at his thin and scraggy sheep, huddled together in the corner of the field, one could almost see in the eyes of these abused and neglected creatures a longing to find themselves under the care of a good and gracious shepherd.

My dear Christian friend – aren't you glad you don't belong to a shepherd like that? You belong to the Good Shepherd. Rejoice in that fact! His care for you will last not only through time, but will go on into eternity also. You will dwell for ever … for ever … in the constant care and loving presence of the Lord.

NATIONAL DISTRIBUTORS

UK (and countries not listed below): CWR, PO Box 230, Farnham, Surrey GU9 8EP. Tel: (01252) 784710 Outside UK (44) 1252 784710

AUSTRALIA: CMC Australasia, PO Box 519, Belmont, Victoria 3216. Tel: (03) 5241 3288

CANADA: CMC Distribution Ltd, PO Box 7000, Niagara on the Lake, Ontario L0S 1JO. Tel: (0800) 325 1297

GHANA: Challenge Enterprises of Ghana, PO Box 5723, Accra. Tel: (021) 222437/223249 Fax: (021) 226227

HONG KONG: Cross Communications Ltd, 1/F, 562A Nathan Road, Kowloon. Tel: 2780 1188 Fax: 2770 6229

INDIA: Crystal Communications, 10-3-18/4/1, East Marredpally, Secunderabad – 500 026. Tel/Fax: (040) 7732801

KENYA: Keswick Bookshop, PO Box 10242, Nairobi. Tel: (02) 331692/226047

MALAYSIA: Salvation Book Centre (M) Sdn Bhd, 23 Jalan SS 2/64, 47300 Petaling Jaya, Selangor. Tel: (03) 78766411/78766797 Fax: (03) 78757066/78756360

NEW ZEALAND: CMC New Zealand Ltd, Private Bag, 17910 Green Lane, Auckland. Tel: (09) 5249393 Fax: (09) 5222137

NIGERIA: FBFM, Helen Baugh House, 96 St Finbarr's College Road, Akoka, Lagos. Tel: (01) 7747429/4700218/825775/827264

PHILIPPINES: OMF Literature Inc, 776 Boni Avenue, Mandaluyong City. Tel: (02) 531 2183 Fax: (02) 531 1960

REPUBLIC OF IRELAND: Scripture Union, 40 Talbot Street, Dublin 1. Tel: (01) 8363764

SINGAPORE: Campus Crusade Asia Ltd, 315 Outram Road, 06-08 Tan Boon Liat Building, Singapore 169074. Tel: (065) 222 3640

SOUTH AFRICA: Struik Christian Books, 80 MacKenzie Street, PO Box 1144, Cape Town 8000. Tel: (021) 462 4360 Fax: (021) 461 3612

SRI LANKA: Christombu Books, 27 Hospital Street, Colombo 1. Tel: (01) 433142/328909

TANZANIA: CLC Christian Book Centre, PO Box 1384, Mkwepu Street, Dar es Salaam. Tel: (051) 2119439

UGANDA: New Day Bookshop, PO Box 2021, Kampala. Tel: (041) 255377

ZIMBABWE: Word of Life Books, Shop 4, Memorial Building, 35 S Machel Avenue, Harare. Tel: (04) 781305 Fax: (04) 774739

For e-mail addresses, visit the CWR web site: www.cwr.org.uk

Bible Classics

£4.99

An attractive and easy-to-read series exploring God's will for our lives, making us the people He has called us to be. These make wonderful gifts for friends and family.

The Lord's Prayer presents one of the most encouraging and instructive passages from the Bible in a way that will inspire enquiring minds. *The Divine Eagle* illustrates how God sometimes pushes us out of our comfortable worlds towards a deeper faith in Him and *The Divine Gardener* shows how God is at work shaping our lives.

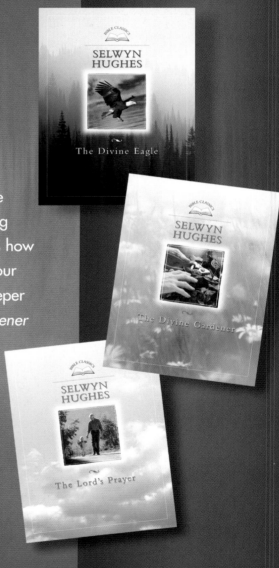

- **The Divine Eagle**
  ISBN 1–85345–190–8

- **The Divine Gardener**
  ISBN 1–85345–191–6

- **The Lord's Prayer**
  ISBN 1–85345–193–2

Pocket Encouragers

This new series offers biblical help, guidance and encouragement. Each title explores various aspects of the Christian experience, such as relationships, Bible study and coping with responsibility. Some content is common to all titles, with unique material that relates especially to men, women, leaders or young adults. Great gifts!

- **Pocket Encourager for Men**
  ISBN 1–85345–177–0

- **Pocket Encourager for Women**
  ISBN 1–85345–178–9

- **Pocket Encourager for Leaders**
  ISBN 1–85345–179–7

- **Pocket Encourager for Young Adults**
  ISBN 1–85345–180–0

£3.99

Favourite Series

This charming series features
best-loved stories, anecdotes,
prayers and illustrations
compiled by Selwyn Hughes
in his 50 years of inspired
ministry. The books present
thoughtful insights and
revealing truths in a
popular and relevant style
for young and old alike.

- **My Favourite Stories about Children**
  ISBN 1–85345–194–0

- **My Favourite Prayers**
  ISBN 1–85345–195–9

- **My Favourite Quotes and Anecdotes**
  ISBN 1–85345–196–7

£3.99

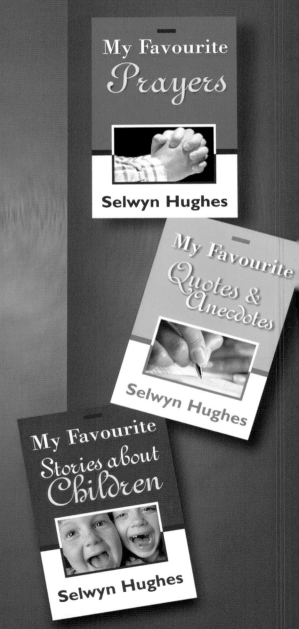